AF375498

Tommy's Sharks Tooth Adventure

Tommy's Sharks Tooth Adventure

Angela Hart Aldridge

AHARTBOOKS

Tommy's Sharks Tooth Adventure

Once upon a time, in a quaint coastal town,
Lived a young boy named Tom, with hair sandy brown.
With a twinkle in his eye and a smile so bright,
He woke up each morning ready for delight.

Tom loved the beach, where the seagulls would cry,
And the waves danced to the tune of the clear blue sky.
But what he loved most, without a single doubt,
was hunting for sharks teeth, scattered all about.

Armed with a trusty bucket and a keen eye,
Tom set off on his quest as seagulls flew by.
He knew every nook, every cranny, every cove,
Where the sharksteeth hid, like treasures trove.

The sun-kissed his cheeks as he strolled the sandy shore,
With the ocean's whispers and the waves' gentle roar.
Each step brought him closer to his prized finds,
For he had a knack for spotting them of all kinds.

Sometimes they gleamed like stars in the sand,
Other times they lay hidden, awaiting his hand.
But Tom was determined, he wouldn't give in,
For sharks teeth, hunting was his favorite kind of win.

As he walked, he imagined the sharks of the deep,
With rows of sharp teeth were secrets they'd keep.
He dreamed of adventures, daring and grand,
Swimming with sharks in a magical land.

But today was different, as luck would have it so,
For on this very day, something special would show.
Amidst the shells and the pebbles, there it lay,
The grandest sharkstooth, to brighten his day.

It glistened in the sunlight, a treasure to behold,
With edges so sharp, it sparkled like gold.
Tom's heart skipped a beat as he held it with care,
This sharkstooth was special beyond compare.

He imagined the shark, mighty and grand,
Swimming through oceans, across every land.
With a grin on his face, Tom whispered a vow,
To protect and cherish this treasure from then until now.

With his bucket now full and his heart full of cheer,
Tom bid farewell to the beach until the next year.
For though the day was ending, the memories would stay,
Of the adventures he had on that fateful day.

So children, remember, as you walk by the sea,
Keep your eyes open for what there might be.
For treasures await in the sand and the spray,
Just like Tom and his sharkstooth, on that special day.

And though the story ends, as all stories do,
The magic of sharkstooth hunting forever rings true.
For in the heart of each child, a treasure does lie,
Just waiting to be found, under the bright sky.

The end.